GW00854850

THE YUMS

Strawberry is beautiful
shiny and red

She doesn't want
to be made into jam

'I have lovely green hair
on top of my head

can't I be eaten just as I am?'

'You can,' Said her
best friend Aubergine

'It isn't out of the question

Pose next to a scone

I'll show you how it's done

People just need
a serving suggestion'

When Strawberry saw him

he looked such a sight

that she let out a
little scream

'Just look at your tummy!

Your nose is so runny

and what have you done with the cream?'

Strawberry gave it a go
and looked mighty fine

with a swirl of cream
on her head

but it covered her hair
so she was filled with despair

'I must try something else
instead'

Strawberries are yummy
dipped in chocolate

so she sat in some melted goo

'This can't be polite
It doesn't feel right

Whatever am I to do?'

Strawberry tried
sitting in jelly

but disappeared
from sight

She nearly drowned
in pink champagne!

She perched on a cupcake
but didn't like the height

so won't try any of those
again!

Strawberry sat down
with Aubergine

not knowing
what else to do

She closed her eyes
and made a wish

then all of her dreams
came true ...

White powder was falling
on Strawberry's head

It fell on her just like snow

She was being sprinkled
with sugar
ready to eat

'Yipee!' She cried
'Here I go...'

Created by Mary Ingram

Read about Strawberry's friends ...

www.theyums.co.uk

Printed in Great Britain
by Amazon

77482681R00018